CIVIL LAW VOCABULARY IN USE

Master 350+ Essential Civil Law Terms And Phrases Explained With Examples In 10 Minutes A Day

JOHNNY CHUONG

Copyright © 2017

All rights reserved.

ISBN: 9781973503880

TEXT COPYRIGHT © JOHNNY CHUONG

all rights reserved. No part of this guide may be reproduced in any form without permission in writing from the publisher except in the case of brief quotations embodied in critical articles or reviews.

Legal & disclaimer

The information contained in this book and its contents is not designed to replace or take the place of any form of medical or professional advice; and is not meant to replace the need for independent medical, financial, legal or other professional advice or services, as may be required. The content and information in this book have been provided for educational and entertainment purposes only.

The content and information contained in this book have been compiled from sources deemed reliable, and it is accurate to the best of the author's knowledge, information, and belief. However, the author cannot guarantee its accuracy and validity and cannot be held liable for any errors and/or omissions. Further, changes are periodically made to this book as and when needed. Where appropriate and/or necessary, you must consult a professional (including but not limited to your doctor, attorney, financial advisor or such other professional advisor) before using any of the suggested remedies, techniques, or information in this book.

Upon using the contents and information contained in this book, you agree to hold harmless the author from and against any damages, costs, and expenses, including any legal fees potentially resulting from the application of any of the information provided by this book. This disclaimer applies to any loss, damages or injury caused by the use and application, whether directly or indirectly, of any advice or information presented, whether for breach of contract, tort, negligence, personal injury, criminal intent, or under any other cause of action.

You agree to accept all risks of using the information presented inside this book.

You agree that by continuing to read this book, where appropriate and/or necessary, you shall consult a professional (including but not limited to your doctor, attorney, or financial advisor or such other advisor as needed) before using any of the suggested remedies, techniques, or information in this book.

TABLE OF CONTENT

INTRODUCTION **5**

ESSENTIAL CIVIL LAW PHRASES AND TERMS **6**

    Section A: 6

    Section B: 15

    Section C: 16

    Section D: 21

    Section E: 24

    Section F: 25

    Section G: 26

    Section H: 27

    Section I: 28

    Section J: 31

    Section L: 32

    Section M: 35

    Section U: 39

    Section N: 40

    Section O: 41

    Section P: 43

    Section R: 48

    Section S: 51

    Section T: 54

    Section V: 62

    Section W: 63

Section Y: 64
CONCLUSION 65
CHECK OUT OTHER BOOKS 67

INTRODUCTION

Thank you and congratulate you for downloading the book *"Civil Law Vocabulary In Use: Master 350+ Essential Civil Law Terms And Phrases Explained With Examples In 10 Minutes A Day."*

With a clear, concise, and engaging writing style, Johnny Chuong will provides you over 350 civil law terms and phrases that help you expand your legal words list with a practical understanding of civil law topics such as *civil rights & obligations, guardianship, civil transactions, estate, lending, types of civil contracts, security for performance of civil obligations, civil liability, invalid civil transactions, inheritance* **and much much more**. If you'd like to increase your wide range of legal vocabulary as well as enhance your knowledge of civil law, then this book may be the most important book that you will ever read.

As the author of the book, Johnny Chuong promises this book will be an invaluable source of legal reference for professionals, international lawyers, law students, business professionals and anyone else who want to improve their use of legal terminology, succinct clarification of legal terms and have a better understanding of civil law and civil procedure. This book provides you with a comprehensive and highly practical approach in legal contexts, the world of civil law related to civil rights, guardianship, civil transactions, security for performance of civil obligations, civil liability, civil contracts, all substantive and procedural aspects of civil law. All legal terms and phrases are well written and explained clearly in plain English.

Take action today and start mastering 350+ essential civil law terms and phrases explained with examples tomorrow!

Thank you again for purchasing this book, and I hope you enjoy it.

ESSENTIAL CIVIL LAW PHRASES AND TERMS

Section A:

A contract: a written or spoken agreement with specific terms for doing something between two or more people.

An employment contract;

A co-operative contract;

A lease contract;

A sale contract.

Authorization: an official permission is given to someone to do something.

Performance of a task without authorization.

The authorization must be made in writing, unless being agreed.

A dispute: a disagreement; a conflict of rights.

A dispute over the rights to a property.

A dispute over land use right.

An adult: a person who is eighteen years of age or older.

Children who are adults but are incapable of working.

Each adult shall have full legal capacity.

A minor: is a person who is under eighteen years of age.

Place of residence of minors.

The place of residence of a minor is the place of residence of his/her parents.

A civil transaction: A civil transaction is a contract or unilateral legal act that gives rise to, or terminates civil rights and/or obligations.

All civil transactions related to the property of a child under six years of age must obtain the consent of his/her legal representative.

A legally incapacitated person: a person who cannot realize or conduct his/her actions as a result of his/her mental or other illnesses.

It is impossible for the legally incapacitated person to take up a job.

A legal guardian: a person who has the legal right or duty to take care of and protect legitimate rights and interests of another person, called a ward.

I thought he was Peter's legal guardian.

Adoptive father: a man who has adopted a child of other parents to raise as his own child.

David is the adoptive father of his wife's two children.

Adoptive mother: a woman who has adopted a child of other parents to raise as her own child.

Peter loved his adoptive mother as if she were his own.

Adoptive parents: a married couple who adopt a child of other parents to raise as their own child.

His adoptive parents has adopted him since 2002.

A natural child = a biological child.

A natural child has the right to change the family name from biological mother's to biological father's or vice versa;

An adopted child: a person that has become the legal child of another parents and has been taken care of as their own child.

An adopted child is treated the same as a natural child.

A transgender person: a person who has a gender identity that differs from his/her birth sex.

Changing of given name of a person whose gender identity is re-determined or a transgender person.

An abandoned child: a child who is left without protection, or care.

An abandoned child whose natural parents are unidentified is adopted.

A non-nationality resident = A stateless person.

He is a non-nationality person.

A remuneration: an amount of money that is paid for work or a service.

A person is eligible for a remuneration if their image is used for commercial purposes.

A violator: a person who breaks or infringe a rule, law or agreement.

When the possession is violated by another person, the individual or through a court compels the violator to terminate his/her violation and compensate for any damage.

A ward: someone who is under the protection of a legal guardian because he/she is unable to manage his/her own affairs.

Wards include:

a) Persons with limited cognition or behavior control.

b) Incapacitated persons;

c) Minors who have lost their mothers and fathers, or whose parents are unidentifiable;

A natural disaster: a natural event such as a flood, tornadoes, earthquake, or hurricane that causes a lot of damage and kills many people.

Thousands of people died in the natural disaster.

A juridical person: entity (such as a company, an organization) other than a natural person (human being) is authorized by law and recognized as a legal entity.

The nationality of a juridical person shall be determined according to the law of the country in which such juridical person was established.

A household: a group of people live together under the same roof and compose a family.

45% of American households used their credit cards to pay for basic living expenses.

A co-operative group: a business that is owned and run together by its members, who share the profits or benefits.

Members of a household, or a co-operative group may agree to authorize another person to enter into and perform a civil transaction related to their common property.

A lease contract: means an agreement between parties whereby a lessor delivers property to a lessee for use during a fixed term and the lessee is required to pay rent.

Lease contracts of houses.

Authorize: to give someone official permission to do something.

Each person may authorize another to enter into and perform a civil transaction.

Authorization: the act of authorizing (official permission to do something).

The duration of the authorization shall be as agreed by the parties or as provided by law.

Authorization contract means an agreement between parties whereby an attorney has the obligation to perform an act in the name of a principal.

A power of attorney: a written authorization to represent or act for another person in specified or all legal matters.

The term of representation shall be determined according to a power of attorney.

An unauthorized person: a person who is not given official permission to do something.

A civil transaction entered into and performed by an unauthorized person representative shall not give rise to rights and obligations of the principal.

Adjacent immovable property: property that is next to another person's property.

Right to adjacent immovable property.

Aquatic animals: animals that live in water.

Keeping stray aquatic animals is considered as the possession with a legal basis.

Possession with a legal basis is the possession of a property in the following case:

A person who discovers and keeps stray domestic animals, poultry or raised aquatic animals.

An emergency circumstance: an event that poses an imminent threat to the life, health, safety of society and the legitimate rights or interests of people.

In an emergency circumstance, the owner and holder of other property-related rights to a property must not hinder another person from using his/her own property or hinder another person from causing damage to such property in order to prevent or abate the greater danger or damage that threatens to happen.

A sale contract: a written agreement between a buyer and seller.

In a sale contract, the seller may remain the ownership of property until the purchaser pays in full the purchase price.

The guarantor: a person or organization who gives a guarantee.

The parties may agree that the guarantor shall only be obliged to perform the obligation if the principal debtor is incapable of performing it.

A lienor: someone who holds a lien on another's property.

The lienor has the right to require the obligor to pay expenses necessary for taking care of and keeping the property.

A bilateral contract: a bilateral contract is a contract whereby each party has an obligation to the other;

The lienor has the right to request the obligor to fulfill completely the obligations arising from a bilateral contract.

A unilateral contract: a unilateral contract is a contract whereby only one party has an obligation;

With respect to a unilateral contract, the obligor must perform the obligation strictly as agreed.

A principal contract: a principal contract is a contract the effectiveness of which does not depend on another contract;

The effectiveness of an ancillary contract will not terminate the validity of the principal contract.

An ancillary contract: an ancillary contract is a contract the effectiveness of which depends on a principal contract;

Invalidity of a principal contract shall terminate an ancillary contract, unless the parties agree that the ancillary contract replaces the principal contract.

A contract for the benefit of a third person: a contract for the benefit of a third person is a contract whereby contracting parties must perform obligations for the benefit of a third person and the third person enjoys benefits from such performance;

An obligee also has the right to demand the obligor perform a contract for the benefit of a third person.

A conditional contract: a conditional contract is a contract the performance of which depends on the occurrence, modification or termination of a specified event.

A conditional contract is also termed as a hypothetical contract.

Appendices to contracts: a section or table of additional terms at the end of the contract.

Appendices providing details on certain terms and conditions of a contract may be attached to the contract.

Amendment or cancellation of contracts: a change made by correction, addition, or deletion of contracts.

Amendment or cancellation of contracts for benefit of third persons.

A recipient: a person who receives or is awarded something.

A giver: a person who gives or awards something to another person.

A giver may require a recipient to perform one or several civil obligations prior to or after the giving of a gift.

A service provider: a company or a person that offers service to others in exchange for payment.

The client has the right to require the service provider to perform the act strictly in accordance with the agreement on quality, quantity, time, location and other matters.

A processor: a person who processes something.

The processor has the obligation to deliver the products to the supplier strictly in accordance with the agreed quantity, quality, method, time and place.

A will = a testament: a legal document by which a person or the testator expresses his or her wishes on how to distribute his or her property after his or her death.

A person may make a will to dispose of his or her estate.

A will must be made in writing. If it is not able to be made in writing, it may be made orally.

An heir: a person who inherit the legacy of a predecessor.

An heir has the right to inherit estate under a will.

A testator: someone who has made a legally valid will or given a legacy.

A testator must write a will by his or her own hand and must sign it.

Alimony: an allowance made to a spouse by the other after a legal divorce.

Disputes over alimonies.

Arbitrator: a person who is appointed to settle a dispute.

Commercial arbitrators.

Appointment or change of arbitrators;

A defense counsel = a trial lawyer.

The defense counsels of the plaintiff's legitimate rights and interests

A defendant: a person or an organization that is sued in a court of law.

If the plaintiff does not know where the defendant resides or works or where his/her head-office is located, the plaintiff may petition the Courts of the area where the defendant last resides or works.

A non-commercial juridical person: a juridical person whose primary purpose is not seeking profits and its possible profits may not distributed to its members.

Non-commercial juridical persons include political organizations, socio-political organizations, social funds, charitable funds, social enterprises and other non-commercial organizations.

Appellate court: a court that has the power to review and overturn decisions made by lower courts.

Court fees shall include first-instance Court fees and appellate Court fees.

Adult children = grown children

The honor, dignity and prestige of a deceased person shall be protected at the request of his/her spouse or adult children/grown children.

Section B:

Bloodline: a set of ancestors of a person includes parents, grandparents, great-grandparents, and so on.

An individual has the right to change the family name when he/she discovers the origin of his/her bloodline.

Body organs: liver, heart, and stomach are examples of body organs.

Right to donate or receive human tissues and body organs and donate corpses.

Biological mother = natural mother = birth mother: the woman who gave birth to a child.

Biological father = natural father = birth father

An individual has the right to change the family name from biological father's to biological mother's or vice versa.

Bona fide: in good faith; without intention to deceive.

Protection of the interests of bona fide third parties with regard to invalid civil transactions.

Business secrets

Business secrets receive strong protection under EU law.

Section C:

Civil law: is a part of a nation's legal system. It includes different areas of law such as labor law, intellectual property law, contract law, family law.

The self-protection of civil rights must be not contrary to basic principles of civil law.

Civil rights: the personal rights of citizens to full legal, social, and economic freedom and equality.

As prescribed in law, civil rights may be limited in exceptional circumstances due to social ethics, social safety and order, and the community's health.

Civil obligations: civil capacity to exercise obligations.

Each person shall be liable for his/her failure to fulfill any civil obligations.

Civil relations: relations established on the basis of independence of property, equality, freedom of will, and self-responsibility.

Each person shall be equal in civil relations.

Civil relations involving foreign elements.

Compensation: money that is paid to someone who has experienced loss or damage.

Compensation for damage.

If any damage has been caused, he/she must also pay compensation.

Contracting parties: Parties that have entered into a legal contract with each other.

Contracting parties of a contract may not disclose information about each other's private life

Co-owner: a person who owns something together with another or others.

… With respect to joint property, the remaining co-owner(s) shall manage the property;

Commercial juridical person: a juridical person whose primary purpose is seeking profits and its profits shall be distributed to its members.

Commercial juridical persons include enterprises and other business entities.

Common property: property owned by two or more people.

Property contributed and created by the members and other property as prescribed by law shall be considered as common property part of the cooperative members.

The common property may not be divided before the termination of the cooperation contract, unless otherwise agreed by all members.

Child custody: physical and/or legal custody of a child.

Mediation and recognition of voluntary divorces and agreements on child custody and property division upon divorces.

Consumable objects and non-consumable objects

A consumable object is an object which loses or is not capable of retaining its original characteristics, appearance and usage after being having been used once.

Consumable objects may not be used as the objects of a lending contract or a lease contract.

A non-consumable object is an object which certainly retains its original characteristics, appearance and usage after being used many times.

Non-consumable objects may be used as the subject matters of a contract for borrowing property.

Cheated person: a person who is deceived or influenced by fraud.

The mistaken or cheated person in a transaction knows and should know that such transaction is established due to misunderstanding or cheating;

Capital contribution: an amount of money or assets given to a business by a partner, owner, or shareholder.

Usually, a capital contribution will be in the form of cash.

Credit institutions: institutions (banks, financial companies) that provide a great variety of financial services.

Escrow deposit is an act whereby an obligor deposits a sum of money into an escrow account at a credit institution to secure the performance of an obligation.

Civil contract: Civil contract means an agreement between parties in relation to the establishment, modification or termination of civil rights and obligations.

A civil contract shall terminate when the contract has been completed or the parties so agree;

Contract for the loan of property: an agreement between parties whereby a borrower is delivered property by a lender.

A contract for the loan of property requires a borrower to perform specific actions.

Contract for lease of property: an agreement between parties whereby a lessor delivers property to a lessee for use during a fixed term and the lessee is required to pay rent.

Unless agreed in contract for lease of property, a tenant may not use the property for commercial purposes;

Cooperation contract: A cooperation contract means an agreement between natural and/or juridical persons regarding the property contribution, effort to perform certain jobs, the same benefit and mutual responsibility.

Contributed property

The member withdrawing from the cooperation contract has the right to reclaim contributed property, divided part of the property in the common property and must pay all obligations under the agreement.

Contracts for services: Contract for services means an agreement between parties whereby a service provider performs an act for a client which pays a fee for that act.

Unilateral termination of performance of contracts for services.

Contracts for transport of passengers: an agreement between parties whereby a carrier transports passengers and luggage to an agreed destination and the passengers must pay transport fares.

A ticket is the evidence of the contract for transport of passengers by the parties.

Contracts for transport of property: an agreement between parties whereby a carrier has the obligation to transport property to an agreed destination and to deliver it to the authorized recipient, and the customer has the obligation to pay the freight charges.

A bill of lading is the evidence of the contract for transport of property by the parties.

Carrier: a person or a vehicle that carries passengers or things.

The carrier has the right to require the passengers to pay in full the passenger transport fares and fares for the transport of personal luggage in excess of the prescribed limit.

Contracts for bailment of property: an agreement between parties whereby a bailee accepts the property of a bailor for safekeeping, for return to the bailor upon expiry of the duration of the contract, and the bailor must pay a fee to the bailee, except where the bailment is free of charge.

Cassation of trials: the act of annulling, or canceling trials.

The Supreme People's Court shall conduct cassation of trials of all Courts;

Civil liability insurance.

The carrier has the obligation to purchase civil liability insurance for the passengers, as provided by law.

Court of first instance: a court in which a legal case is first heard.

The first-instance judgments or decisions.

The first-instance judgments or decisions of the Courts can be appealed against under the provisions of the Civil Code.

Section D:

Declaration of birth

Declaration of death

Right to declaration of birth and death.

Deposit: an amount of money that you pay as the first installment on the purchase or rent of something.

Deposit is an act whereby one party (the depositor) transfers to another party (the depositary) a sum of money or other valuable things for a period of time as security for the entering into or performance of a contract.

Withdraw deposit funds.

Dependent: an individual who relies on another individual, especially a family member, for financial support.

He has four dependents to support.

Divisible objects and indivisible objects.

A divisible object is an object which retains its original characteristics and usage after being divided.

A divisible object can be divided into portions for the purpose of performing a civil obligation.

An indivisible object is an object which is not able to retain its original characteristics and usage after being divided.

The indivisible object must be valued in money for the purpose of division when it needs to be divided.

Deception: the action of deceiving somebody.

Deception in a civil transaction means an intentional act of a party for the purpose of misleading the other party as to the subject or contents of the civil transaction which has caused the other party to enter into such transaction.

Derelict property: property that is abandoned by the owner.

The police went to a nearby derelict property and found the handbag.

Damage: detrimental effects on someone or something.

If damage is caused, compensation must be made.

Destroyed property: property that is completely ruined or does not exist any more.

When property is destroyed, the ownership rights with respect to such property shall terminate.

Damaged property: property that is spoiled, harmed or ruined.

Cancellation of the contract in the case of lost or damaged property.

The violating party shall compensate in cash equal to the value of damaged property.

Delivery of property: the action of delivering the property.

Place for delivery of property.

Method for delivery of property.

Section E:

Equality: the state of being equal, particularly in rights, obligations and opportunities.

The right to equality between husband and wife.

Ethnicity: a particular ethnic group (shares a common culture, religion, and language).

Each person has the right to identify and re-identify his/her ethnicity.

Existing property: property that exists now.

Existing property means a property which is formed before or at the time of transaction establishment.

Effectiveness = validity = in effect.

The forms of civil transactions shall be the conditions for its effectiveness.

Escrow deposit: Escrow deposit is an act whereby an obligor deposits a sum of money, precious metals, gems or valuable papers into an escrow account at a credit institution to secure the performance of an obligation.

Evidences and proof in civil procedures

The collection of evidences and proof must be carried out sufficiently.

Section F:

Freedom of will: the ability to act at one's own discretion; voluntary decision.

Self-responsibility: the state of being responsible for his/her own behavior.

Property rights and obligations of each person in civil relations are established on the basis of equality, freedom of will, and self-responsibility.

Financial obligations: an amount of money that a person must pay to another at a particular time for his/her debt.

Deduct a portion from the property of the absent person in order to perform the obligations of such person to pay due debts or financial obligations.

Force majeure: unforeseeable events that prevent a person from fulfilling a legal agreement.

An event of force majeure is an event which occurs in an objective manner which is not able to be foreseen and which is not able to be remedied by all possible necessary and admissible measures being taken.

Fidelity guarantee: a type of insurance purchased by an employer who wants to protect against business losses.

Fidelity guarantee is a type of security for the performance of obligations.

Section G:

Given name = First name.

Family name = Surname.

Each person has right to have a family name and a given name.

Guarantee: Guarantee means an undertaking made by a third person to an obligee to perform an obligation on behalf of an obligor if the obligation falls due and the principal fails to perform or performs incorrectly the obligation.

All civil rights are guaranteed under the Constitution and law.

Gemstones: a jewel or stone used in jewelry.

Diamonds are the most lasting of all gemstones.

Guardianship: a person who is required by law or appointed to take care of and protect legitimate rights and interests of another person who is unable to manage their own affairs.

The guardianship must be registered by law.

Section H:

Health insurance: a type of insurance coverage that provides compensation for medical and surgical expenses.

There are different costs associated with health insurance.

A pension for old age, and accident and health insurance, should be provided.

Human's rights: the fundamental rights that are believed to belong justifiably to all human beings.

Many people think that Capital punishment is cruel and it is against human's rights for life.

Health facility: places that provide health care such as hospitals, clinics, etc.

A person who discovers a situation where another person has a life threatening accident or illness, he/she must take such person to a nearest health facility;

Section I:

Immovable property: property that cannot be moved such as land or buildings.

Movable property: property which is not immovable property.

Property includes immovable property and movable property.

Illegal use of assets.

Illegal use of assets is not tolerated.

Intellectual property rights: the legal ownership by a person over the creations of their minds.

The intellectual property rights shall be determined in accordance with the laws of the country in which the objects of the intellectual property rights are required to be protected.

Inheritance: the act of inheriting something (money or property).

A will shall become legally effective at the time of commencement of the inheritance.

Invalidity: the fact of not being valid.

Invalid civil transactions.

An invalid civil transaction shall not give rise to, change or terminate any civil rights and obligations of the parties as from the time the transaction is entered into.

In good faith: sincerely and honestly (in an honest way).

Possession in good faith.

Possession in good faith means the possession that the possessor has bases to believe that he/she has the right to the property under his/her possession.

Initiating legal action

Limitation period for initiating legal action claiming compensation for damage.

Intentional fault: Intentional fault means that a person is fully aware that his or her act will cause damage to another person but still performs the act and, irrespective of whether or not it so wishes, allows the damage to occur.

Unintentional fault: Unintentional means that a person does not foresee that his or her act is able to cause damage, even though he or she knows or should know that the damage will occur.

Fault in civil liability includes intentional fault and unintentional fault.

Initiate civil lawsuits

The plaintiff has the right to initiate civil lawsuits against the defendant when he or she has been harmed by violations of the defendant's act.

Illegal marriages: the establishment of husband and wife does not conform to the legal restrictions of a marriage prescribed by law;

The Courts of the areas where illegal marriages are registered shall have the jurisdiction to resolve petitions to revoke such illegal marriages;

Illegal strike: a strike that is called in violation of law.

Disputes over compensation for illegal strike.

Inheritance right: the right to inherit something (money or objects).

Inheritance right of individuals.

Interpretation: the act of interpreting or explaining the meaning of something.

Interpretation of civil contracts.

Misunderstanding: a failure to understand something correctly.

A misunderstanding in a civil transaction.

Invalidity of civil transactions due to misunderstanding.

Deception: the act of deceiving someone.

Threat: a situation when a person says that they will cause someone harm or problems, especially if he or she does not do what they tell him or her to do.

Compulsion: the action of forcing someone to do something;

Invalidity of civil transactions due to deception, threat or compulsion.

Section J:

Joint ownership: Joint ownership means multiple ownership whereby each owner's share of the ownership rights with respect to the multiple ownership property is not specified.

Joint ownership includes divisible joint ownership and indivisible joint ownership.

Joint obligation: Joint obligation means an obligation which must be performed by more than one person.

Joint obligation on a loan.

Justice: the process of using laws to fairly judge and punish criminals.

Protect the justice.

Social justice cannot be attained by violence.

Joint property: property that is owned by two or more people.

Multiple ownership property by a community is indivisible joint property.

Section L:

Legal personality: legal entity; a person, a corporation or an organization that has legal rights and obligations.

All individuals shall have the same legal personality.

Legal prohibitions: provisions of law which do not permit entities to perform certain acts/ the action of forbidding something by law.

Invalidity of civil transactions due to breach of legal prohibitions.

Liability: the sums of money or debts that someone owes.

The liability for property.

Lender: a person or an organization that lends money.

The lender must deliver the property to the borrower in full, strictly in accordance with the quality and quantity, and at the time and place, agreed.

Lien on property: Lien on property means that the obligee who is legally possessing the property being an object of a bilateral contract is entitled to retain the property when the obligor fails to perform the obligations or has performed the obligations not strictly as agreed upon.

If the obligor failed to perform the obligation at the due time, lien on property shall arise.

Lease: a contract by which the owner of a property (a building, a piece of land) coveys it to another for a specified time, usually in return for money.

A three-month lease on an apartment; lease contracts of houses.

A consumable object may not be the object of a lease contract.

Lease terms = the terms of a lease.

The term of a lease shall be as agreed by the parties. If there is no agreement, the term of the lease shall be determined according to the purpose of the lease.

Legal capacity: the legal right of an individual or corporation to make particular decisions, or to have particular obligations/ the capability to establish and exercise civil rights and perform civil obligations.

Each adult shall have full legal capacity.

People with limited legal capacity must have a defense counsel in the trial.

Legal representative: A person who represents the legal affairs of another.

The court shall appoint a legal representative of the person with limited legal capacity.

Lack of legal capacity: the condition of not being able to realize or conduct someone's actions as a result of his/her mental or other illnesses.

Due to his lack of legal capacity, he was unable to object to the payment order related to the sale of his house.

Land use right = Right to use land.

Contracts relating to land use rights must be made in writing.

Legally effective judgments and decisions of Courts.

Legally effective judgments and decisions of Courts must be enforced and strictly observed by all agencies, organizations and individuals.

Section M:

Mediation = reconciliation: the action of mediating between parties.

The Courts have the responsibility to conduct mediation and create favorable conditions for the involved parties to reach agreement with one another.

Make a payment: an amount of money that someone must pay.

The purchaser is obligated to make a payment to the seller.

Method of payment: a way someone pays for a transaction.

The parties reach an agreement with clear terms about price and method of payment.

Marriage status.

Regardless of the marriage status, all children have the same rights and obligations to their parents.

Mixed multiple ownership: Mixed multiple ownership means ownership of property in respect of which owners from different economic sectors contribute capital for the purpose of conducting production and business for profit-making purposes.

The possession, use and disposal of property under mixed multiple ownership must comply with laws relating to capital contribution;

Marital property: Property acquired by either spouse during their marriage.

A husband and wife shall discuss, agree on or authorize each other in relation to the possession, use and disposal of the marital property.

Multiple ownership property: an ownership type system where property can have at least two owners.

Each of the owners in common has rights and obligations with respect to the multiple ownership property corresponding to its share of the ownership rights.

Mortgage: the act of giving property to a creditor (a bank or similar organization) as security on a loan in order to buy a house.

A mortgage is a kind of loan that people can use to buy a house.

Mortgage of property means the use by one party of property under the ownership of the obligor as security for the performance of an obligation to the other party.

A mortgage of property shall terminate when the obligation which is secured by the mortgage has terminated;

Missing person: a person who has disappeared and there is no reliable information on whether such person is still alive or dead even though notification and search measures have been fully applied.

He has been reported as a missing person.

Management of the property.

The guardian has the right to receive payment of all necessary expenditures on management of the property of the ward.

Maintenance: the act of maintaining or preserving something.

A lessee shall take care of leased property as if it were its own and shall carry out minor repairs and maintenance.

Market price: the price of a good or service when is offered in a given market.

When parties reach no agreement about the rent, it shall be determined according to the market price at the time and place of entering into the contract.

Mistaken person: A person who is wrong about someone's opinion or something.

Movables: estates; property that can be moved (do not include land or buildings).

Civil transactions related to movables required registration.

Mental illnesses: a disease of the brain with disorders that affect your emotions, thoughts and behavior.

GAD is a mental illness that causes someone to feel anxious regularly.

Medical examination and treatment.

Law on medical examination and treatment.

Medical treatment: the treatment and care given to a patient to combat disease.

Each individual has the right to receive tissues and/or body organs of other persons for his/her medical treatment.

Section U:

Unilateral termination of performance of the contract: termination of performance of the contract by one person or party.

Unilateral termination of contracts for transport of passengers.

Unilateral termination of performance of processing contracts.

Unilateral termination of performance of authorization contracts.

Unlawful: illegal; not permitted by, or recognized by law.

Obligations to return property due to unlawful possession.

Unlawful: illegal; not permitted or recognized by law.

Unlawful decision; unlawful possession.

Unilateral: performed by only one person or one party without the agreement of the others.

A unilateral legal act; a unilateral contract.

Usufruct right: Usufruct right means the right to use a property, under ownership of another entity, and enjoy its yield or income in a specific period of time.

The usufruct right shall be established from the time of transfer of the property.

Section N:

National interests: the interests of a nation as a whole.

The establishment and performance of civil rights and obligations shall not infringe national interests, legitimate rights and benefits of other people.

National defense = National security

Civil rights may be limited as prescribed in law in exceptional circumstances that due to national defense and security.

Notarization: the act or process of notarizing by a notary.

Notarization is essential for official documents including contracts, mortgages, etc.

Nationality: The status of belonging to a particular nation by birth.

Each person has the right to nationality.

Section O:

Occupational diseases: any chronic ailment that happens as a result of work or occupational activity.

Treatment cost for occupational accidents or occupational diseases.

Ownership right: the rights of an owner to possess, use and dispose of a property.

Real estate: property in the form of land or buildings, or things permanently attached to land and buildings.

Civil transactions related to real estate are required registration.

Ownership in common: Ownership in common is multiple ownership whereby right of ownership shared by two or more entities with respect to the multiple ownership property is specified.

Multiple ownership comprises ownership in common and joint ownership.

Oral argument: The spoken legal presentation to a judge by the attorneys before a court.

Oral will: a will that is communicated verbally to witnesses.

Where a person is likely to die due to illness or any other reason and it is not possible for him or her to make a written will, such person may make an oral will.

The obligor is not able to perform a civil obligation due to an event of force majeure.

Objective hindrance: An objective hindrance is a hindrance which results in a person with civil rights or obligations not knowing that his or her lawful rights and interests have been infringed or not being able to exercise his or her rights or fulfill his or her civil obligations;

The time when the objective hindrance or force majeure occurs shall not be included in the payment term.

Off-plan property: if you purchase an off-plan property that means you buy it before it is built.

Off-plan property includes non-formed property and formed property.

Immovable property and movable property may be existing property or off-plan property.

Ownership: the right of possessing something/ legal possession of something.

Ownership rights comprise the rights of an owner to possess, use and dispose of the property of the owner.

Section P:

Possessor: a person who owns something.

Possession in good faith means the possession that the possessor has bases to believe that he/she has the right to the property under his/her possession.

If there is a dispute over the rights to a property, the possessor of such property shall be presumed to have those rights. The disputing person must prove that the possessor have no right.

Place of residence

The place of residence of an individual is the place where such person usually lives.

Personal rights: Personal rights are the rights that a person has over their own body and cannot be transferred to other persons.

Personal rights not associated with property.

Personal rights associated with property.

Property: a thing or things that belong to someone/ property comprises objects, money, valuable papers and property rights.

Manage the property of the absent person/ expenditures on management of the property of the absent person.

Pledge: the act of giving property to another as security on a debt/loan.

She left her car as a pledge that she would return with the money.

Property rights: Property rights are rights which are able to be valued in money.

Property comprises objects, money, valuable papers and property rights.

Property comprises objects, money, valuable papers and property rights.

Performance of joint obligations

An obligation which shall be performed by at least two persons.

Personal secrets

She is very good at keeping personal secrets.

Precious metals: gold, silver, and platinum.

Security collateral is an act that a lessee of a property transfers precious metals, a sum of money or other valuable things to the lessor for a specified time limit to secure the return of the leased property.

Post-divorce child custodian.

Disputes over change of post-divorce child custodian.

Petition: a formal written request to a higher authority.

Petitions for consideration of legitimacy of a strike.

Pay the freight charges.

The customer must pay the freight charges for transporting the property to the place agreed in the contract.

Processing contracts: processing contract means an agreement between parties whereby a processor carries out work to create products at the request of a supplier, and the supplier receives the products and pays fees.

Upon termination of the processing contract, the processor must return leftover raw materials to the supplier unless otherwise agreed.

Possession: the act of having or owning something/ a person holds and controls a property directly or indirectly as holder of rights to such property.

Possession includes possession of owners and possession of non-owners.

Property with unidentified owners: objects of which owner is unidentified.

Possession with a legal basis is the possession of a property with unidentified owners.

Stray domestic animal: a domestic animal that has strayed.

Poultry: domestic fowl, such as birds, chickens, ducks, and geese.

An individual who discovers and keeps stray aquatic animals, domestic animals, or poultry will have the right to possess such animals with a legal basis.

Professional secrets

The young man had to pay a fine of over $50,000 after he admitted to disclosing professional secrets.

Pledge of property: Pledge of property means the delivery by one party of property under its ownership to another party as security for the performance of an obligation.

Agreement on pledge of property shall be valid from the time of concluding.

The pledged property

The pledgee must have the obligation of taking care of and preserve the pledged property.

Physical damage: tangible damage to a property that adversely affects the use, or value of such property.

The physical damage means those actual physical losses, comprising loss of property, reasonable expenses to prevent, mitigate or restore damage, and the actual loss or reduction of income.

Preserve the property: to take care of the property in order to prevent it from being harmed or destroyed.

The mortgagee has the right to require the mortgagor to apply necessary measures to preserve the property and the value of the property.

Private property: The ownership of something, especially land or buildings by an individual who has exclusive rights over it.

He does not have private property or sufficient private property to make the payment.

Possession not in good faith: means that the possession that the possessor knew or should have known that he/she has no right to the property under his/her possession.

Primary objects and auxiliary objects

A primary object is an independent object the utility of which can be exploited according to its functions.

An auxiliary object is an object which directly supports the exploitation of the utility of a primary object.

Section R:

Reasonable costs: costs which are reasonable.

Reasonable costs for the prevention, mitigation and remedy of the damage;

Retain the property: to keep in possession of the property.

She can retain the property until the other party renders performance.

You can retain the property and sue for damages for his breach of contract;

Lien on property means that the obligee who is legally possessing the property being an object of a bilateral contract is entitled to retain the property when the obligor fails to perform the obligations or has performed the obligations not strictly as agreed upon.

Lien on property shall arise from the due time that the obligor failed to perform the obligation.

Registration of security: the registration of security shall comply with the law on registration of security.

Registration of security over a right under a contract.

Registration of security by overseas companies.

Renunciation of ownership rights: the formal rejection ownership right of something.

The renunciation of ownership rights must comply with the law.

Right to use: Right to use means the right to exploit the usage of, and to enjoy the yield and income derived from, property.

Right to use land for cultivation

Rights of an individual with respect to his/her image

Each individual has rights with respect to his/her own image.

Renounce ownership right: to give up the ownership right of something.

The right to renounce ownership/ Renounce ownership right is a part of the owner's general right of disposition over the property.

Right of disposal: right of disposal means the right to transfer ownership rights, renounce ownership rights, right to use, or destruct the property.

Right of disposal of owners.

Right of disposal of non-owners.

The right of disposal of property, including retention of ownership and retention of the right to sell the property.

Right to life, right to safety of life, health and body.

Each individual has the right to life, the inviolable right to life and body, the right to health protection by law.

Reclaim property: to take back property that was yours.

If the buyer fails to fulfill the payment obligation for the seller as agreed, the seller is entitled to reclaim the property.

Right to protection of honor, dignity and prestige.

Honor, dignity and prestige of an individual is inviolable and protected by law.

Section S:

Spousal common property: property owned by a married couple.

Spousal common property during their marriage.

Disputes over division of spousal common property during their marriage.

Summon: to call or notify someone to appear in a court of law.

To summon a defendant.

Request the court to summon witnesses.

Social ethics: are common standards of conduct that are recognized and respected by the whole community.

The purpose of the civil transaction shall be not contrary to the law and social ethics.

Spouse: someone's husband or wife/ a person that someone is married to.

Property relations between spouses shall be dealt with the Law on marriage and families.

Surface rights: surface rights mean an entity's rights to the ground, water surface, space thereon and earth bowel of the land whose land use rights belong to another entity.

Each holder of surface rights has the right to exploit and use ground, water surface, space thereon, the water and the earth bowel of the land.

Other property-related rights include right to adjacent immovable property, usufruct right, and surface rights.

Social ethics: Social ethics are common standards of conduct as between persons in social life, which are recognized and respected by the community.

Invalidity of civil transactions due to contravention of social ethics.

Security collateral: Security collateral is an act whereby a lessee of a movable property transfers a sum of money or precious metals, gems or other valuable things to the lessor for a specified time limit to secure the return of the leased property.

Security collateral is a property or other valuable things that a borrower offers a lender to secure a loan.

Service supplier: a person or organization that provides a product or a service.

The processor has the obligation to take care of the raw materials supplied by the supplier.

Settlement of civil cases

Many people are paying as much attention to the settlement of civil cases as they are to the trial.

Settlement of civil cases by mediation is gaining ground in the Supreme Court although mediation is not compulsory.

Spiritual damage: spiritual damage means losses related to life, health, honor, dignity or reputation and other personal benefits of an entity.

At the request of the obligee, a court may compel the obligor to pay spiritual damages to the obligee.

Self-protection: protection of oneself or property against some damage caused by another.

Self-protection of civil rights.

Severance pay: an amount paid to an employee upon the early dismissal or discharge from employment.

The employees were offered 10 weeks' severance pay.

Social insurance: form of compensation provided by a government for the elderly, the disable, or the unemployed.

Sex reassignment.

The sex reassignment shall comply with regulations of law.

Section T:

To appeal: to make a formal request to a higher court to review the decision of a lower court.

The decisions to recognize the involved parties' agreements may be appealed against according to the cassation procedures.

The appellate judgments or decisions

Within 15 days as from the day on which the appellate judgments or decisions are issued, the appellate Courts must forward the judgments and/or decisions to the Courts which conducted the first-instance trials.

The mortgaged property: Mortgage of property means the use by one party of property under the ownership of the obligor as security for the performance of an obligation to the other party without transferring such property to the mortgagee.

Regarding mortgage on land use rights that property on land is owned by the mortgagor, such property shall also part of the mortgaged property.

The mortgaged property shall be held by the mortgagor.

The mortgagor has the obligation to transfer documents related to the mortgaged property to the mortgagee.

Transfer of ownership rights: Make over the possession of (property or land) to another.

Transfer of ownership rights by owner to the buyer.

Threat or compulsion in a civil transaction means an intentional act of a party which compels the other party to conduct the civil transaction in order to avoid danger to the life, health, honor, reputation, dignity and/or property or that of its relatives.

The people's ownership: Property under the people's ownership include land, water resources, mineral resources, resources in the waters, airspace and other natural resources.

The deceased person = dead person: someone who has recently died.

At the request of his/her spouse or grown children, the honor, dignity and prestige of a deceased person shall be protected by law;

To notarize: to legalize or certify (a document, contract, etc.) by a notary.

A contract for the exchange of property must be made in writing, and must be notarized.

The birth certificate: an official document issued to record the name, date and place of a person's birth.

The family and given names of a person shall be recorded in the birth certificate of such person.

The right to private life, personal secrets and family secrets.

The private life, personal secrets and family secrets of a person are inviolable and protected by law.

The right to marry or divorce.

Each person has the right to marry or divorce.

The right to acknowledge father, mother or child.

Each person has the right to acknowledge father, mother or child in marriage relation.

The right to adopt children and be adopted in marriage relation.

Each person has the right to adopt children and be adopted in marriage relation.

To destroy: to damage to something that it does not exist anymore.

Ownership rights terminate when the property is consumed or destroyed.

To terminate: to bring to an end; to end or stop.

Terminate the civil rights and obligations.

Terminate a civil transaction.

The lawful rights and interests = the legitimate rights and interests

A person may not use his/her pen name to cause damage to the legitimate rights and interests/ the lawful rights and interests of other people.

A guardian is responsible for protecting the legitimate rights and interests of the ward.

To revoke: to officially state that a law, decree, agreement or decision is no longer in effect.

Revoke the decision.

A testator may amend, replace or revoke his will at any time.

To infringe: to break or fail to obey the terms of a law, or an agreement.

The exercise of civil rights and obligations shall not infringe lawful rights and interests of other people.

The court's decision.

Her lawyer said the court's decision wasn't correct and that she should file for an appeal.

Termination: the act of bringing something to an end; the act of terminating.

The termination of the act of violation.

Termination of ownership rights.

The act of violation: the act of breaking or infringing a law, agreement, etc.

The termination of the act of violation.

The consent: permission, approval, or agreement for something to happen.

The use of an image of a person must have his/her consent.

To consent: to give permission or approval/ to permit or agree for something to happen.

All civil relations relating to personal rights of a minor shall be established and performed with the consent of his/her legal representative.

The borrower: a person or an organization that borrows money.

When the loan is due, the borrower must repay the property of the same type, and must pay interest if so agreed to the lender.

The obligor = the obligated party: A person who owes an obligation (a payment or duty) to another by contract or other legal agreements.

The obligor must perform the obligation strictly in accordance with the relevant time-limit.

The exploitation of the property: the act of making use of and benefiting from the property.

The value of benefits from the exploitation of the property shall be offset against the value of the obligation of the obligor.

Transfer of risks: risks of loss are transferred to another party through a contract.

The seller shall bear all risks of the property or goods until the property or goods is delivered to the buyer.

Transport costs = the costs of transportation.

Transport costs and costs related to transfer of ownership rights.

The performance of the contract for the land use rights must follow the procedures prescribed by the law of the land.

The aggrieved party: a person whose financial, personal, or property rights or interests are directly affected by a decree, judgment, or statute.

To pay a fine: an amount of money that someone must pay as a punishment for breaking a law or rule.

Agreements on fines for violations are reached by the parties to a contract which requires the violating party to pay a fine to the aggrieved party.

The trial use: used in a test of the quality of something that is done for a specified period of time to see if it is worth buying, or using.

The trial use of purchased property.

During the trial use period, the purchaser may inform the seller whether or not the purchaser wishes to make the purchase.

The litigator: The litigator in a civil lawsuit is the person that initiates lawsuit.

Litigators are customers who are not required to prove faults of organizations and individuals trading goods and/or services.

The civil lawsuit: a lawsuit based on disputes between persons or organizations, such as disputes involving contracts.

Before the opening of the trial, the Judges who are assigned to resolve the civil lawsuits shall be competent to issue decisions to suspend/resume/terminate the resolution of such civil lawsuits.

The bailor: the person who entrusts his/her property to another person.

The bailee: the person to whom personal property is bailed.

The bailor must pay a fee to the bailee for safekeeping the property of the bailor.

To inherit: to receive (a right, property, or a title) as an heir at the ancestor's death.

Peter inherits an expensive house left to him under his father's will.

The plaintiff: the party who initiates a lawsuit against another in a court of law.

He is the plaintiff in that trial.

The court rules in favor of the plaintiff.

Termination of cooperation contract.

A cooperation contract shall terminate in any of the following cases:

a) As agreed by cooperative members;

b) The purpose of cooperation has been achieved;

The service fee: an amount of money that is paid for a particular service.

If there is no agreement on the service fee rate, the service fee rate shall be fixed on the basis of market fees for services of the same type at the time when and place where the contract was entered into.

The violating party: the party that break, infringe or fail to comply with a rule or an agreement.

The parties may reach an agreement that the violating party has to pay only a fine for violations has to pay both a fine for violations and a compensation for damage.

The offeror: someone who makes an offer to another to enter into a contract.

When the offeror modifies the contents of the offer, that offer shall be deemed to be a new offer.

A contract is considered to be entered into since the offeror receives the reply accepting to enter into the contract.

The offeree: a person who receives an offer to enter into a contract.

Offer to enter into a contract means a clear expression by the offeror of its intention to enter into a contract and to be bound by such offer made to another specific party or the public (hereinafter referred to as the offeree).

If the offeror fails to enter into the contract with the offeree and the offeree suffers damage, the offeror must compensate the offeree for such damage.

The termination of the cooperation contract.

The common property may not be divided before the termination of the cooperation contract, unless otherwise agreed by all members.

Acceptance of an offer to enter into a contract means a reply by the offeree to the offeror accepting the entire contents of the offer.

Section V:

Voluntary divorces.

Any person requesting for recognition of voluntary divorces and agreements on child custody and property division upon divorces must submit petitions.

Valuable papers: A special type of property.

Property comprises objects, money, valuable papers and property rights.

Section W:

Written will: a will that has been entirely handwritten and signed by the testator.

Written wills comprise:

1. Unwitnessed written wills;

2. Witnessed written wills;

3. Written wills which are notarized;

4. Written wills which are certified.

Witnesses: a person who sees or observes an event.

Warranty obligations: a written guarantee, given to the purchaser by the manufacturer, promising to repair or replace the product if necessary within a particular period of time.

In addition to demanding the performance of warranty obligations, a purchaser has the right to require the seller to compensate for damage caused during the warranty period due to technical defects of the object.

Section Y:

Yield and income

Yield means natural products brought by property.

Income means a profit earned from the development of the property.

When a civil transaction is invalid, the bona fide party who receives yield or income is not required to return such yield or income.

CONCLUSION

Thank you again for downloading this book on *"Civil Law Vocabulary In Use: Master 350+ Essential Civil Law Terms And Phrases Explained With Examples In 10 Minutes A Day."* and reading all the way to the end. I'm extremely grateful.

If you know of anyone else who may benefit from the essential Civil Law terms and phrases explained with examples that are revealed in this book, please help me inform them of this book. I would greatly appreciate it.

Finally, if you enjoyed this book and feel that it has added value to your work and study in any way, please take a couple of minutes to share your thoughts and post a REVIEW on Amazon. Your feedback will help me to continue to write other books of IELTS topic that helps you get the best results. Furthermore, if you write a simple REVIEW with positive words for this book on Amazon, you can help hundreds or perhaps thousands of other readers who may want to improve their legal vocabulary so that they could get the greatest achievements in work and study. Like you, they worked hard for every penny they spend on books. With the information and recommendation you provide, they would be more likely to take action right away. We really look forward to reading your review.

Thanks again for your support and good luck!

If you enjoy my book, please write a POSITIVE REVIEW on Amazon.

-- Johnny Chuong --

CHECK OUT OTHER BOOKS

Go here to check out other related books that might interest you:

Legal Vocabulary In Use: Master 600+ Essential Legal Terms And Phrases Explained In 10 Minutes A Day

http://www.amazon.com/dp/B01L0FKXPU

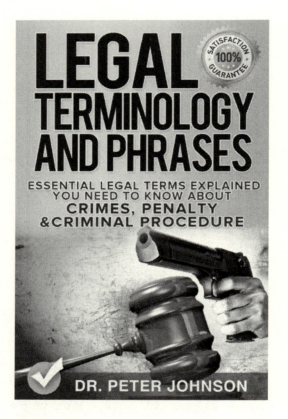

Legal Terminology And Phrases: Essential Legal Terms Explained You Need To Know About Crimes, Penalty And Criminal Procedure

http://www.amazon.com/dp/B01L5EB54Y

Ielts Writing Task 2 Samples : Over 450 High-Quality Model Essays for Your Reference to Gain a High Band Score 8.0+ In 1 Week (Box set) https://www.amazon.com/dp/B077BYQLPG

Ielts Academic Writing Task 1 Samples: Over 450 High Quality Samples for Your Reference to Gain a High Band Score 8.0+ In 1 Week (Box set) https://www.amazon.com/dp/B077CC5ZG4

Shortcut To English Collocations: Master 2000+ English Collocations In Used Explained Under 20 Minutes A Day (5 books in 1 Box set)

https://www.amazon.com/dp/B06W2P6S22

IELTS Writing Task 1 + 2: The Ultimate Guide with Practice to Get a Target Band Score of 8.0+ In 10 Minutes a Day

https://www.amazon.com/dp/B075DFYPG6

IELTS Speaking Strategies: The Ultimate Guide With Tips, Tricks, And Practice On How To Get A Target Band Score Of 8.0+ In 10 Minutes A Day.

https://www.amazon.com/dp/B075JCW65G

Shortcut To Ielts Writing: The Ultimate Guide To Immediately Increase Your Ielts Writing Scores.

https://www.amazon.com/dp/B01JV7EQGG

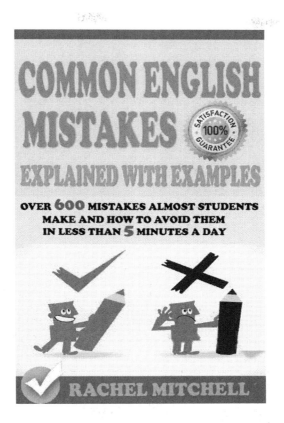

Common English Mistakes Explained With Examples: Over 600 Mistakes Almost Students Make and How to Avoid Them in Less Than 5 Minutes A Day

https://www.amazon.com/dp/B072PXVHNZ

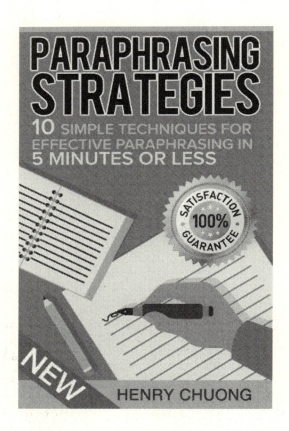

Paraphrasing Strategies: 10 Simple Techniques For Effective Paraphrasing In 5 Minutes Or Less

https://www.amazon.com/dp/B071DFG27Q

Productivity Secrets For Students: The Ultimate Guide To Improve Your Mental Concentration, Kill Procrastination, Boost Memory And Maximize Productivity In Study

http://www.amazon.com/dp/B01JS52UT6

Daughter of Strife: 7 Techniques On How To Win Back Your Stubborn Teenage Daughter

https://www.amazon.com/dp/B01HS5E3V6

Parenting Teens With Love And Logic: A Survival Guide To Overcoming The Barriers Of Adolescence About Dating, Sex And Substance Abuse

https://www.amazon.com/dp/B01JQUTNPM

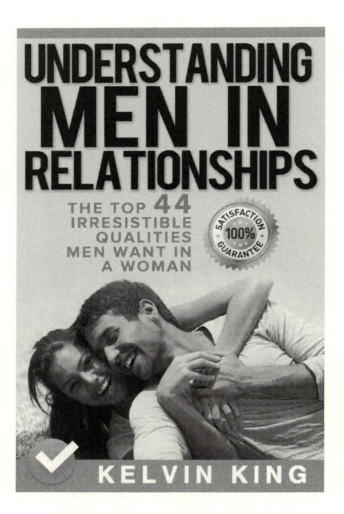

http://www.amazon.com/dp/B01K0ARNA4

Made in the USA
Middletown, DE
30 July 2019